INSIDE THE INDUSTRY
THE ARTS

BY A. M. BUCKLEY

INSIDE THE INDUSTRY
THE ARTS

BY A. M. BUCKLEY

Content Consultant
Cynthia L. Favre
Director of Career Management
Gustavus Adolphus College

ABDO
Publishing Company

CREDITS

Published by ABDO Publishing Company, 8000 West 78th Street, Edina, Minnesota 55439. Copyright © 2011 by Abdo Consulting Group, Inc. International copyrights reserved in all countries. No part of this book may be reproduced in any form without written permission from the publisher. The Essential Library™ is a trademark and logo of ABDO Publishing Company.

Printed in the United States of America,
North Mankato, Minnesota
112010
012011

 THIS BOOK CONTAINS AT LEAST 10% RECYCLED MATERIALS.

Editor: Holly Saari
Copy Editor: Paula Lewis
Interior Design and Production: Christa Schneider
Cover Design: Christa Schneider

Library of Congress Cataloging-in-Publication Data
Buckley, A. M., 1968-
  The Arts / by A.M. Buckley.
     pages cm. -- (Inside the Industry)
  Includes bibliographical references.
  ISBN 978-1-61714-797-5
  1. Arts--Vocational guidance--Juvenile literature. I. Title.
  NX163.B83 2011
  700.23--dc22
                              2010042449

TABLE OF CONTENTS

If you love taking art classes, a career in the arts industry may be for you.

IS AN ARTS JOB FOR YOU?

"Art is an end to the question 'what is it?' or 'what does it mean?'"[1]

—*Keith Haring (1958–1990), graffiti artist*

Ever since you were little, you've been the one exploring art, painting or drawing, taking pictures or making collages,

IS AN ARTS JOB FOR YOU?

dancing or dreaming. You've always loved art, and now you're starting to consider your future and the big question: What do you want to do with your life? You're pretty sure it will have something to do with art, but what? You want to explore some of your options.

OVERVIEW OF THE ARTS INDUSTRY

The arts industry encompasses the many expressions of art, including dance, film, painting, sculpture, photography, and many more. The creative professionals who work in these fields make their livings by working with their imaginations to create images, sounds, performances, or ideas that showcase these creations. These people use their skills, imagination, and unique ideas to entertain, teach, motivate, and inspire.

People who choose to pursue the arts tend to be independent thinkers who want to communicate and participate in culture. They understand that beauty, ideas, and imagination are vital to happiness, growth,

NUMBER OF ARTISTS

The number of artists in the United States has grown steadily over the years, nearly tripling since 1970. According to "Artists in the Work-force: 1990–2005," a report by the National Endowment for the Arts, 2 million Americans are artists and approximately 40 percent of these are designers. Los Angeles County is the most popular home for artists—as many as 141,000 artists live there. In close second is New York City, home to 133,000 artists.[2]

and innovation. Artists make and build, dance and draw, communicate and reflect—not because they are guaranteed a steady job or because someone has told them to, but because they recognize, believe in, and value the benefits of art.

The arts industry offers a wide variety of jobs, some of which are overlooked when people consider the arts field. Even in related fields—design and advertising, film and fashion—there are still more creative professions. Designers make Web sites, furniture, books, and bags. Filmmakers make movies; actors perform in films and on the stage. Fashion designers invent new styles of clothing and shoes. Motion graphics artists create visual effects for films and television. Set designers arrange the scenes for a theater or a movie set. There are so many ways to turn your imagination and ingenuity into a career in the arts.

"Everything pays dividends except dreaming—dreaming softens you and makes [you] unfit for daily work. It is difficult to be an artist and close the door to dreams."[3]

—Louise Bourgeois (1911–2010), artist

WHAT'S IT LIKE TO WORK IN THE ARTS?

Art is a fascinating business because people do not need art in the same way they need food, water, or housing. Even people who love art do not buy it every day or even every year. Arts professionals balance busy and productive times with quiet periods of focus and hard work, financial successes with economic downturns.

While some artists gain immense recognition during their lifetimes, it is very rare. Many artists have exhibitions to show and sell their art, but they are not famous. In fact, most artists have a secondary form of work, often in the arts, to help support themselves and their families. For example, many artists also work as teachers or professors. Curators may double as art writers, and some dancers work as choreographers.

Because art is such a popular field, it can be a challenging field to break into. However, if you love art and want to be around it, there seems to always be a way, but it requires considerable dedication and commitment.

EMPLOYMENT AND WAGE STATISTICS

According to the Bureau of Labor Statistics *Occupational Outlook Handbook, 2010–2011 Edition*, approximately 60 percent of artists are self-employed.[4] Most find some additional form of work with magazines, museums, schools, or other arts organizations. Annual wages for arts professionals vary widely. They range from approximately $32,000 to $88,000, but pay can be significantly more or less than these figures depending on the career and the market.[5]

A PASSION FOR ART

Being in the arts is a calling and a way to expand one's mind, heart, and spirit. Whether a professional is creating, showing, or selling art, people that choose this field have a passion for art and expression—just like you.

ARTS AS A POSITIVE INFLUENCE

Young artists often help their communities in positive ways. Research shows that young artists are four times as likely to do volunteer work or community service and are less likely to be involved in delinquent behavior. They are also four times as likely to join youth groups and twice as likely to read for pleasure—an indication of academic success.[7]

Many arts professionals feel they would find a way to work in the arts no matter what. They have a sense that they are meant for the arts—whether it is to make art or write about it, take pictures, dance, or organize exhibitions. As Blythe Camenson stated in *Careers in Art*, "Successful artists might tell you that they never consciously chose a career in the art—the profession chose them."[6]

Dancing is one possible career path to explore in
the arts industry.

TEN POPULAR JOBS IN THE ARTS

Are you ready to explore which arts jobs are good fits for you? An artist, a dancer, a photographer, and a curator are only a handful of the plethora of jobs in the arts industry. Other popular jobs in the field include:

1. Choreographer: Choreographers create original dances to be performed in a variety of dance styles and settings ranging from ballet to musical theater and music videos to commercials. Most choreographers begin as professional dancers.

2. Owner of a Dance Studio: Dance studios are places where dance is taught and performed. Some dancers open their own studios to teach classes and own their own businesses.

3. Teacher of Art, Dance, or Photography: Teachers in the arts are responsible for passing on history, technique, and inspiration to students of all ages. Most teachers specialize in one area, such as painting or jazz dance.

4. Professor of Art or Dance: Professors teach in a college or university setting. Art or dance professors have specialized knowledge in particular areas of the arts and possess higher education degrees in their fields.

5. Art Conservator: Art conservators have specialized training in art conservation and restoration. They examine and treat art objects and artifacts so the works will not be damaged over time.

6. Preparator: Art preparators handle works of art for installation and, when necessary, for shipping. They have knowledge of hanging and arranging art and prepare works for exhibitions.

7. Archivist: Archivists normally work in museums with large collections of art. Their job includes overseeing the cataloging that keeps track of each item in the collections.

8. Creative Director: Creative directors orchestrate the look or design of a particular endeavor. This can include commercials, public art, and design projects.

9. Arts Administrator: Arts administrators are in charge of arts organizations and facilities that include arts educational groups and performing arts centers. Administrators run daily operations and often raise funds for their organizations.

10. Arts Writer or Critic: Arts writers contribute articles about the arts to magazines and newspapers. Critics specifically write reviews of exhibitions or performances.

The arts industry holds abundant opportunities for a variety of career paths. This book offers insight into some of these paths, offering in-depth explanations of jobs and tips for how to get there.

Artists use their imaginations to create works for several reasons: for purely aesthetic purposes, to inspire viewers, and when commissioned by others.

WHAT IS AN ARTIST?

In general, artists make things that other people will view, usually in galleries or museums, but sometimes in public places, such as corporate offices or hospitals. Their creations inspire people to think, feel, imagine, or reflect. Many artists

14

work with traditional media, such as painting, drawing, and sculpture. But art can—and increasingly is—made from any material imaginable.

Artists spend their time developing and expanding on their unique practice, whether it is a particular style of painting or sculpting, a form of collage, photography, film or video, or a combination of different media. Artists tend to focus on one idea or type of media, such as oil paints or screen prints, color and light, or poetry and metaphor, but this can change as artists grow and develop.

"We artists should not underestimate the importance of the stories we tell ourselves about how art will make a difference."[1]

—David Humphrey, artist and writer

When developing their creations, artists determine what to make and how to make it. When creating works requested by employers, clients, or patrons, the artist usually still controls how to interpret and display the content. However, a client may sometimes dictate an art piece, which can take out much of the creativity for the artist.

Most artists make and exhibit work regularly. Artists who work in two-dimensional, such as painting or video, or three-dimensional work, such as sculpture, are also called visual artists. This distinguishes them from dancers or performing artists. A working artist refers to a living artist who is actively developing and exhibiting his or her work.

WHAT IS AN ARTIST'S WORK ENVIRONMENT?

Rather than work at jobs with scheduled hours for specified amounts of time, artists often set their own schedules. Some artists prefer to work at night; others work better during the day. Artists' schedules depend on personal preferences as much as on the materials they work with and their need to earn an income. Once they have an idea, artists can spend long hours executing works.

Artists generally work in studios, but studios vary widely. A studio can be a room in a house or an apartment, a garage, or a rented warehouse or loft. Artists' studios depend on the type of work they do and the space and equipment required.

ARTIST STUDIOS

Sarah Thornton, author of *Seven Days in the Art World*, noted, "A studio is supposed to be a site of intense contemplation." When Thornton visited the internationally renowned Japanese artist Takashi Murakami at his studio, he explained that he worked "anywhere, anytime. . . . I take a deep breath, send oxygen to my brain, meditate for a few seconds, and get to work."[2]

HOW IS THE JOB MARKET FOR ARTISTS?

Most artists do not earn a living solely from their artwork. A few artists earn enough money from art to get by. At the highest level of the art market, some artists earn millions of

Some artists use their art to convey social
or political messages.

dollars, but this is rare. In their book *Art/Work*, Heather Darcy
Bhandari and Jonathan Melber wrote,

> Every artist has a day job (almost). We're not just talking
> about MFA grads at the beginning of their careers, but
> successful artists at big-city galleries. . . . So don't buy into
> the myth that you're not a good artist, or a successful artist,
> or a "real" artist, if your art doesn't pay the bills.[3]

Some artists work in the art world, taking jobs in galleries
and museums or teaching art. Sometimes artists work in
the commercial art industry. Still others have jobs that use

completely different skill sets. These can vary widely from waitress to attorney.

Because so many artists earn a living in another way, apart from selling their art, it is very difficult to determine the average income for working artists; however, in 2008, the Bureau of Labor Statistics reported that the median annual wage for artists working in fine art was $42,650.[4] The authors of Art/Work reported,

> The average income of an artist at an emerging gallery, from sales of artwork, is less than ten thousand dollars a year. The big-name artists selling work for hundreds of thousands of dollars are a tiny fraction of the art world.[5]

Commercial artists use their creativity and skills in the service of making movies, television shows, advertising, illustration, or various forms of web or industrial design. In 2008, the Bureau of Labor Statistics estimated that art directors earned an annual median wage of $88,510 and multimedia artists earned a median of $62,380. The Department of Labor predicts an increase over the next few years in the need for artists that work with multimedia.[6]

A PROFILE OF AN ARTIST

Like many artists, Dane Picard had been working with his hands and making art for most of his life. As a child, he took apart radios and other electronics to understand how they were made, often rebuilding them in new ways. Growing up, he experimented with different kinds of drawing and painting, including charcoal and oil.

However, it was not until his early twenties that Picard decided to pursue a career as an artist. Transferring out of the electrical engineering program at the University of Utah, Picard moved to Seattle. He received his undergraduate degree from the Cornish College of the Arts, where he became very interested in video art. He continued his education to receive a graduate degree.

Picard then pursued work in visual effects in the film industry while starting his career as an artist. He worked his way up from visual effects technical director to computer graphics supervisor, and he continued to make drawings and videos whenever he could. But Picard wanted to pursue a career as an artist more seriously. He stepped back from his work on films and focused on making art and finding a gallery and other exhibition venues.

> "Being an artist is a role in society that informs tomorrow while looking at yesterday and today—at its best, art inspires people to do great things."[8]
>
> —Dane Picard, artist

Today, Picard makes electronic sculptures by repurposing materials from found and store-bought electronics. His work is exhibited in national and international exhibitions, including those at the Pasadena Museum of California Art, Austin Museum of Art, Torrance Art Museum, and Richard Heller Gallery. On being an artist, Picard said, "I have the opportunity to explore anything through art, and I decide what I'm exploring."[7]

For Picard, the biggest challenge to being an artist is balancing a career in the arts with making money. Picard advised young artists, "Make sure that you learn some skills that people will hire you to do so that you can make money in ways other than just selling your art."[9]

A DAY IN THE LIFE OF AN ARTIST

A typical day in the life of an artist varies greatly. One of the best things about being an artist is the freedom to create, not only one's work, but also one's schedule. In addition to making art, a typical day might involve seeking out places to exhibit work. This is a time-consuming process and tends not to be a favorite part of the job for most artists. To be considered by a gallery or a museum, artists need to prepare presentations with high quality images of their work and information about education and previous exhibitions.

Artists could also spend time applying for other opportunities. These

ART GALLERIES AS AGENTS

Artists do not have agents, but galleries function somewhat similarly. Artists do not need to have galleries to show or sell work, but galleries can help artists develop their careers. Galleries represent a group of artists, meaning that they support the artists' work by exhibiting it in the gallery and showing the work to collectors and curators. Artists are not required to pay a fee to the gallery, but they must be accepted for representation. Galleries generally take 50 percent of any sales they make of an artist's work.

Artists' studios and workshops can range from small rooms in their homes to large warehouse spaces.

can include grants and residencies. Artists also attend exhibition openings, lectures, and get-togethers to meet and network with others in their field.

When an artist has an upcoming exhibition, much of his or her time may be spent completing artwork. But the artist also needs time to meet with the curator or gallery director to decide on how the works will be installed, create a press release, set prices for the works, and promote the show.

TOP FIVE QUESTIONS ABOUT BECOMING AN ARTIST

1. *Can I be an artist?*

    There is no official test to pass or governing body to decide who is an artist. Anyone can call himself or herself an artist. But to have a career as an artist, it is important to explore your work in a serious way and make it the best that you can, learn about the art business, and find opportunities to show your work.

2. *How would I show my work?*

    More established artists may research galleries not only in their own cities but in large cities around the world, such as New York, Los Angeles, Paris, London, and Berlin. But, young artists are likely to start with smaller, local venues. They contact art dealers or send their materials to galleries for review and hope for a positive response. Artists who research galleries to find one that is a good fit with their work have the best chance for success.

3. *What is the difference between fine art and commercial art?*

    Fine art usually has no purpose beyond its own presence and ability to incite ideas, emotions, and commentary or perspective on the world. Commercial art, on the other hand, is made in industries that use creative ideas and talents for other purposes such as entertainment, profit, or advertising.

4. *How could I use my artistic skills to supplement my income?*

    Artists with backgrounds in writing can earn additional income as arts writers or critics. Artists with skills in photography, design, or computer graphics often earn extra money by working in design or advertising. Artists skilled in animation and computer graphics may find work in the visual effects industry. And a great many artists draw on their experiences to teach at schools or universities.

5. *How long would it take me to become an artist?*

    Being an artist is a lifelong journey. While a person can be an artist at any age, the most successful artists visualize their career as a long-term process, taking steps toward their goals along the way. In today's art market, young artists and recent graduates can achieve success early, but gallery directors, curators, and experienced artists tend to caution young artists to take their time. The pressure to be successful and a fully developed artist at an early age may be intense, but try to stay patient and let your work develop naturally.

Being in an art club can broaden your art skills and increase your opportunities to learn about art.

WOULD YOU MAKE A GOOD ARTIST?

What does it take to be an artist? An artist needs to be creative and imaginative, but it takes more than that to be successful. Here are additional characteristics and skills that lead to great artists.

BELIEF AND PASSION

Being an artist is a way of life. It can be filled with adventure and passion, joys and successes, but it can also be a lonely pursuit. On good days and bad, through exhibitions and quiet times, artists continue to develop their work, even if no one is around to see it. For many artists, this is the best part of the process; they enjoy creating art. But when artists struggle to get by, down times can also bring doubts and insecurities. Artists continue because they are passionate about their art.

"Find something that is really meaningful to you—that's the most important thing at the end of the day."[2]

—*Charles Long, artist*

PERSONAL MOTIVATION

Being an artist is usually not the kind of job where someone tells you what to do and how to spend your day, so artists need to be independent and self-motivated. Because most artists work on their own, in their studios and in forging a new path for themselves and their art, they tend to be independent thinkers who seek inspiration for themselves. As artist Dane Picard stated, "A good artist needs the courage to look deep into themselves and persevere when encouragement isn't forthcoming."[1]

FLEXIBILITY

Today's artists have to be flexible about the way they work. This includes developing their style and work and in making a living. If you like adventure and change—and work well in a variety of situations—being an artist will be easier for you than if you prefer stability and routine.

OPEN TO REJECTION

Artists have to apply for all kinds of opportunities, and they inevitably get rejected. Artist and photographer Heather Cantrell stated, "It takes courage and you have to be strong and be open to rejection. Get comfortable with rejection, but don't take it as a negative thing."[3]

RESILIENCY

Because artists make things that other people will see, they often hear opinions about their work. Some of these are positive and some are negative. The most successful—and happy—artists listen to opinions to get a sense of what their art is communicating, but they don't get bogged down in negative criticisms. However, artists should seek out opinions of those other than their family and close friends. Objective feedback is crucial for growth as an artist.

MARKETING SKILLS

Artists who have or develop some form of marketing skills tend to have more success in exhibiting and selling their work. Artists often network and negotiate with others to get their artwork displayed. An entrepreneurial spirit, self-discipline, and self-management can go a long way on the business side of being an artist.

CHECKLIST

Is a career as an artist a good fit for you? Discover if you've got what it takes by answering these questions:

- *Do you have a passion for art?*

- *Do you enjoy creating things?*

- *Do you often express yourself and your ideas visually?*

- *Do you dream of being an artist—or are you one already?*

- *Do you have an adventurous spirit?*

- *Are you adaptable to different situations?*

- *Do you handle criticism and feedback well?*

- *Are you self-motivated and independent?*

- *Do you get an idea of something you want to do or make and find a way to proceed with it?*

If you answered yes to most of these questions, you are on track for a career as an artist. Even if your responses do not seem to fit the kind of personality or skills described in these chapters, a career as an artist could still be right for you. Hard work and determination can go a long way in helping you achieve your dream job.

Seeking feedback and constructive criticism from teachers and peers is a good way for artists to improve.

HOW TO GET THERE

CLASSES TO TAKE IN HIGH SCHOOL

Taking any kind of art course is valuable. Even if you prefer sculpture and do not like painting or photography, knowing about all kinds of art is extremely useful. Drawing, in particular, is an important skill for all artists. Knowing how to draw will allow you to communicate your ideas—whether for sculptures, public projects, or art installations.

Courses in history, humanities, and sciences will help you learn more about the world around you. In turn, this can fuel and inspire your development as an artist. A good understanding of math is important for artists who often work on a freelance basis or as independent contractors, since these jobs include developing prices and charging clients for services.

COLLEGE COURSES

Though you can find examples of successful artists who did not go to college, more and more often, today's artists attend college and graduate school. You'll need to decide if you want to major in art or if you want art to be a hobby outside of academics. Artists have chosen both routes, so you will need to find the best path for you.

College and graduate-level courses in art history, film studies, cultural theory, and media will provide you with a broader understanding of the field and some of the art created throughout history. You will also learn about society's

GROWTH RATE FOR ARTIST JOBS

According to the Bureau of Labor Statistics, employment of artists and arts-related workers is expected to grow 12 percent through 2016. This is about average job growth.[4]

rejections and receptions of those works. Depending on your art medium and subjects, courses in anatomy, geometry, and physics could help you learn more about the human body, shapes, and movement. It is also important to take courses that interest you. A course might inspire your art or lead to a job that supports your art. All the while, continue to develop your art by taking different art courses.

INTERNSHIPS

Another possibility is to pursue an internship or volunteer position at an art gallery or a museum. Internships are becoming the first professional job for college students. Internships may be paid or unpaid opportunities to work with organizations on their operations or projects. Internships provide a way to get hands-on experience and knowledge of how the arts world operates. Working with experienced artists and arts-related professionals also provides opportunities to learn the variety of ways artists engage in their art and earn a living.

"Unlike gold or diamonds, art has this other value, and that's what makes it fascinating. Everything else is trying to sell you something else. Art is trying to sell you yourself. That's what is different about it. Art is what makes life worth living."[5]

—Keith Tyson, artist

VOLUNTEERING

Volunteering is one way to get the experience needed to qualify for an internship. It can be challenging to land a volunteer position, but be patient. Start by learning as much as you can about the place where you want to volunteer. Exploring the facility's Web site and visiting the facility are good ways to start. Attending events at the museum or the gallery is a great way to learn what the facility offers and ways that you might be able to volunteer.

VIEW AND STUDY ART

One of the most important ways to grow as an artist is to view art. Go to gallery and museum exhibitions. Look at works that interest you and those that do not interest you. Try to consider what artists were aiming to achieve in different works. When you do not understand something, read about it or ask an employee in the gallery if he or she can help you understand it. Sometimes the works you like least will teach you the most.

SEEK A MENTOR

An invaluable resource for an artist is having a mentor. Perhaps through volunteering, interning, or art studies, you will find an artist who works in your medium, whose work you admire, or who you feel a special connection with. Ask that person if he or she would be your mentor. A mentor can provide you with feedback on your art, give you advice about the industry, and teach you new ways of creating or expanding your art.

"If you go into it knowing that you will probably not be rewarded lavishly, but you can in fact continue to work, you're on a much better footing than if you go into it trying to make a huge impact when you're 23 or 24, and then maintain that for the next 60 years."[6]

—Robert Storr, critic, curator, and dean of the Yale School of Art

JOIN AN ART CLUB

Perhaps there is a youth group or community center with an arts group. Or maybe there is an arts club at your school. If there isn't, try starting one. Together with your peers, you can create exhibitions, read books and magazines about art, and form discussion groups to share the art you make. You can gain experience as an artist and show your passion, commitment, and initiative.

Budding artists must have passion to create art and express themselves, but they must also be persistent and self-motivated.

Sometimes, dancers must evoke strong emotions
in their performances.

WHAT IS A PROFESSIONAL DANCER?

Movement is universal—almost everyone all over the world dances in some way or another, whether for a long time or at a specific event. This is one thing that makes dance special; everyone can share in it. But even though nearly everyone can dance, only professionals choose to make dance their career.

A professional dancer expresses ideas, stories, emotions, and experiences in movement. To do it well, it takes years of commitment, practice, and perseverance. It means sticking with dance even when you do not get applause or payment, when you are tired and sore, and when you do not feel like dancing. But the rewards of being a professional dancer are many for those who love to dance. A professional dancer has the great opportunity of turning a passion into a career.

> "The story begins with my mother taking me to see the *Nutcracker* when I was two years old and my saying, 'I want to dance, Mommy!' I have been dancing since then. About two years ago, an opportunity presented itself and my father helped me open my dance studio."[1]
>
> —Jennifer Weigand-Watkinson, dancer and owner, Dance Express LLC

WHAT IS A PROFESSIONAL DANCER'S WORK ENVIRONMENT?

A professional dancer is often a member of a dance company. A dance company is a group of dancers who work and perform together, generally under the direction of one choreographer or artistic director. Companies tend to emphasize a particular form, such as ballet or modern, and have a unique style or vision. Other dancers work on a freelance basis, meaning they dance for a particular job or show for a set amount of time.

Being a professional dancer is a social career. Dancers spend hours each day with other dancers, practicing choreography and movements. However, dancers often practice alone as well. Professional dancing also often involves travel, adventure, and the opportunity to perform for audiences around the world.

HOW IS THE JOB MARKET FOR PROFESSIONAL DANCERS?

If you love to dance, being able to do it all day is not a chore, but a pleasure. And being paid to dance is a wonderful experience. But like all creative jobs, dancing is competitive. Often hundreds of dancers try out for a few parts.

Pay rates for dancers, like other artists' jobs, vary widely, but the Bureau of Labor Statistics reported in 2008 that the median hourly rate for dancers was $12.22. The median hourly rate for choreographers was approximately $20.[2] A dancer in a dance company averages approximately $38,520 per year. Some companies pay dancers more, and the principle dancers are usually paid more than other dancers in the company.[3]

DANCE EMPLOYMENT

The majority of prominent US dance companies are located in New York, but almost every state has at least one dance company, and its dancers perform across the country. Approximately 14 percent of professional dancers are self-employed. They work on jobs dancing for operas, television shows, movies, music videos, and commercials.

The Department of Labor predicts that jobs will grow more slowly in dance than in other industries. However, an increase is expected in the number of jobs for dance teachers.[4]

A PROFILE OF A PROFESSIONAL DANCER

When she was eight years old, Elaine Wang started ballet. At first she did not like it much, but her mother encouraged her not to give up too easily. Within a year or two, Wang had fallen in love with ballet. But it was hard at times. "I was always the last one to be booted up into the next level," she recalled, "but I slowly kept going by being diligent."[5]

Wang's slow and steady pace paid off. She was accepted to study dance at Julliard, the primary performing arts academy in the United States, where she studied for one year. She then transferred to the University of California Los Angeles (UCLA) to dig more deeply into what was leading her toward a life of dance. After taking classes on dance history and philosophy, she found her answers. She said,

> I remember taking these classes and being asked new kinds of questions, such as why people make art, is art valid, and do artists have a responsibility in society. This was the first time I [had] ever thought about these things. It was after that class that I really knew I wanted to be a dancer.[6]

Wang completed her studies at UCLA and started dancing professionally. For six years, she danced with two companies and taught dance classes. She decided to go to

Dancers in a company spend a lot of time together in practices and performances.

graduate school for her master's degree at Tisch School of the Arts in New York. After graduation, Wang continued to dance professionally, eventually starting her own company, with which she traveled to New York, Los Angeles, and San Francisco.

What Wang loves most about dance is the social interaction it involves and its capacity for creative expression. She stated, "You get to know people in ways they don't expose to outside worlds. You have to because you share weight, constantly problem-solve, and have to trust and synchronize."[7] Of the expressive possibilities of dance, she added, "Words can be beautiful and potent, but movement can capture so many shades and nuances of a feeling or of a thought."[8]

TAKING CARE OF YOUR BODY

"Take care of your body when you're young, forming good habits like nutrition and warming up and cooling down. . . . Try to think about the process rather than acquiring that perfect shape and learn to understand your body and how it functions. There are things you aren't going to be able to do today, but you'll be able to do them later."[9]

—*Elaine Wang, dancer, choreographer, dance teacher*

As of 2010, Wang performs and choreographs modern dance. She also teaches at the new Central High School for the Arts in Los Angeles, sharing her passion for the art form with her students.

A DAY IN THE LIFE OF A PROFESSIONAL DANCER

A dancer in a company typically spends the entire day dancing. For example, a dancer might take a morning class to maintain technique. In the afternoon, the same dancer works with the other members of the dance company, creating a new dance, developing skills and movement partnerships, or practicing for a performance. In the evening, if there is no performance, the dancer might rest or take another class for fun or to improve form.

When a company is performing, its dancers follow a similar schedule. But during this time, evenings are filled with dress rehearsals and performances. These are followed by spending time with the public and other dancers; talking with members of the press, the audience, or patrons; and gathering with dancers from the company and others in the field. If the company is on tour, the dancers' lives are also filled with travel to new places, practice in foreign lands, and performances for new audiences. When dancers go on tour, their room and food expenses are paid for, and they often receive overtime pay.

"I'm from a small town of about 10,000 people in Slovenia and was literally recruited off of the soccer field! It was thought I had good coordination and rhythm. I found myself being in modern dance class with 18–19 year-old girls and myself, a 10-year-old boy!"[10]

—Tadej Brdnik, dancer in the Martha Graham Dance Company

Aspiring dancers must spend long hours practicing and perfecting technique.

TOP FIVE QUESTIONS ABOUT BECOMING A PROFESSIONAL DANCER

1. *How would I find a job?*

   Dancers take classes and get to know others in their community. They learn about auditions through word of mouth, advertisements, or based on the recommendations of teachers. Dancers work in dance performances but can also be hired for music videos, commercials, musical comedies, or other types of performances that include dance. A dancer usually works on one job at a time but continually auditions to keep working.

2. *How do I know if I'm good enough for a dance career?*

   Dancing is extremely competitive and only those with the highest skill levels succeed. These dancers have worked and studied many hours a day for many years. If you really love dance, keep practicing and believing in yourself. If you aren't able to earn an income dancing professionally, perhaps you will teach dance or develop a new style of dance.

3. *Is there an age limit for professional dancers?*

   Although there is no official age limit for professional dancers, opportunities to perform decrease with age. The majority of professional dancers first audition around age 17 or 18. They perform through their twenties and thirties, but they then often feel the pull of age in their bodies and are hired for fewer roles.

4. *What are some ways I could supplement my income as a dancer?*

    Like artists, many dancers maintain a second job to support themselves. Dancers often work as dance teachers in community centers, dance studios, high schools, or colleges. Some dancers study and teach another form of movement, such as yoga or Pilates; others learn and practice movement therapy, massage, or acupuncture. Some dancers work in arts administration, and others start dance companies or work as choreographers.

5. *Is it realistic to hope for a career in dance?*

    Professional dancing, like all jobs in the arts, is extremely competitive, and there are not enough openings for all the dancers that seek these positions. Some dancers perform in other ways, including in operas or on television shows. Others start their own dance companies, work as choreographers, or teach. If you really love dancing, continue practicing and learn to understand your strengths, your style, and what's important to you. Then you can create a career in dance that works for you and fits your skills.

If you want to be a professional dancer, you will have to work very hard—but remember to have fun!

WOULD YOU MAKE A GOOD PROFESSIONAL DANCER?

You love to dance—in your room, on stage, in the dance studio—but do you have what it takes to have a career as a dancer? Having a few key traits and skills makes it more likely that dancing is the path for you.

44

PASSION FOR DANCE AND PEOPLE

Dancers who truly love dancing and can commit to it wholeheartedly will be the most successful and happy as professional dancers. Like artists, dancers must be self-motivated, but unlike the more solitary work of the visual artist, dancing is more social. It involves partnership and collaboration through classes, performances, and dance companies. Choreographers often call upon dancers to create movements to express ideas, so a good dancer is creative and works well with others to make a successful performance.

DANCE UNIONS

Union membership can offer protections, such as sick leave and a minimum wage, to dancers who are under contract. The American Guild of Musical Artists is the main union for ballet and modern dancers. The Actors Equity Association covers dancers in theatrical performances, such as musical comedies. The American Guild of Variety Artists covers dancers in variety shows, such as the Rockettes. The Screen Actors Guild, which covers actors and actresses in the film industry, also protects dancers who perform in movies.

ENERGETIC AND FIT

Being a professional dancer is physically demanding. Dancers must be strong, flexible, and graceful. Dancers usually dance an average of eight hours a day to stay in top form and to practice for performances. This requires stamina and a great amount of physical training. Though a variety of body types are celebrated in dance, professional dancing still requires intense physical fitness and skill.

DISCIPLINE, PERSEVERANCE, AND ADAPTABILITY

In a highly competitive field, dancers must work extremely hard at their craft, sometimes without a lot of feedback or support. Good dancers are disciplined in both mind and body. Rejection is likely, but in order to make a career, dancers must take rejection in stride, keep practicing, and keep auditioning. They must be able to listen to feedback of their dancing and use it positively to improve, rather than just rejecting criticism outright. Good dancers are also adaptable. Dances often integrate multiple forms and styles, including jazz, modern, and ballet. Dancers who are willing to try new things and learn new forms have a higher chance for success.

A BIT OF ADVICE

Amy Marshall is the choreographer and artistic director of the Amy Marshall Dance Company. On starting out as a choreographer and founding a dance company, she advised, "Don't forget to have a sense of humor and try not to take things too personally. Meet each challenge and move on without getting a chip on your shoulder. The rewards will come, but they take time. You must build integrity before you get praise."[1]

46

Professional dancing can be found in several genres, including ballroom dance, ballet, and modern dance.

CHECKLIST

There is no single formula to becoming a dancer or creating a career in dance, whether in ballet, tap, jazz, modern, folk, or another genre. But the following questions will help you understand if you have the ability, stamina, and commitment to become a professional dancer.

- *Do you love to dance?*

- *Are you physically fit? If not, are you willing to do the work to get there?*

- *Do you enjoy expressing yourself through movement?*

- *Do friends see you as expressive, graceful, or particularly skilled at movement?*

- *Do you have a lot of energy?*

- *Are you social and outgoing?*

If you answered yes to most of the questions, you are probably well inclined for a career in dance. But even if you answered no to some, the important thing is to get to know yourself, what you are good at, and where you have strengths. Then you can use these to help you decide if you want to be a dancer, and if so, what kind of dance to pursue, or if you want to work in another field and dance on your own time.

HOW TO GET THERE

TAKE CLASSES

If you have not started studying dance yet, but know that you want to, there's never a better time to start than the present. Although you may already dance around your home or with friends, dance training is required. Sign up for dance classes at your school or take them at a local community college. You can ask teachers and friends if there is a local dance studio or community center where you can take classes.

Professional dancers, particularly those in ballet, start out at a very young age. But take the classes that interest you and do not be discouraged. Perhaps the ballet class you dreamed about taking, but that was not a very good fit for you, will lead you to something else down the road. Also, there are many other kinds of dance, including folk and ethnic. Keep an open mind and try any style of dance that comes your way; you never know which one might be the perfect vehicle for you to grow, express yourself, and help you create a career in dance.

DANCE, DANCE, DANCE

The most important thing you can do to become a dancer is to dance. Because most dancers start at a young age, you may already have been

STARTING AGE FOR BALLET

Although female ballet dancers generally start young, between the ages of five and six, male ballet dancers can start a little later, between the ages of ten and 15.

dancing for many years. In that case, it is important that you not only continue to dance but you also get to know yourself and your body. This includes trying to understand what form or style of dance you are most suited for and perhaps taking classes in different kinds of dance or simply trying to find your own voice and creativity within the form you currently study.

EXPLORE

Learning about professional dance, including understanding what different companies are like and how each functions, is an important part of knowing where you would fit in best as a professional. John Michael, a ballet dancer, advised, "Most major ballet companies have second companies that resemble an internship. Find the company/choreographer that you want to work with and see if they have a second company."[2]

EDUCATION

Education is important to professional dancers. In addition to studying dance, you can benefit from taking classes in the life sciences, such as biology, physiology, and kinesiology. These can expand your understanding of the body and movement and help you appreciate the complex system of the body. Along with this, it is very wise for dancers to study some form of health education, including nutrition, particularly taught by a teacher who understands dancers' concerns.

Other courses helpful to dancers include dance history, choreography, and classes in other art forms and the humanities. Learning about events and people in history and various cultures can inform and inspire artists' work. Movement is universal, but recognizing the diversity of humanity is important for dancers who interpret a variety of emotions and experiences.

In the past, most dancers went straight from high school into auditions. There are certainly dancers who take this route today. But, more and more dancers choose to attend college and even graduate school. A degree in higher education gives dancers more opportunities outside of dancing. And studying in college is also a way to meet choreographers and other dancers. Oftentimes, while these dancers are in school, they are trying out for and working in dance roles, too.

> "To me, what makes a good dancer is when they are thinking, when their every movement has purpose. You can see that one thing leads to another; there is a reaction and a process and they are not just repeating something but asking, what do you have to say with this movement? That's where the artistry and voice come into dance."[3]
>
> —*Elaine Wang, dancer, choreographer, dance teacher*

BE INVOLVED IN THE DANCE COMMUNITY

Whether you have been dancing for a long time, or want to start now, it's a good idea to get involved in the dance community. Taking classes and workshops is a great way to meet other dancers and learn about auditions. Attending dance performances helps you learn about dance and see dance at a professional level. Some of these events are very expensive, but be on the lookout for community dance troupes or school dance performances, which are more accessible. Any way you can practice, watch, and learn about dance will help you on your way. And you never know what might lead to a new path or a big break.

A good work ethic, energy, and discipline are key characteristics a professional dancer must have.

Some professional photographers focus solely on wedding photography.

WHAT IS A PROFESSIONAL PHOTOGRAPHER?

A photographer uses a camera to create an image that captures a story or a moment or conveys an idea. Today, cameras are readily available on cell phones and in computers, and most everyone can be a photographer. But professional photographers develop their skills and vision over time and take photographs for a living. A professional photographer needs creativity, technique, and the right equipment to take high quality photographs.

Some photographers make images their art form, taking pictures for exhibitions or for books. As with other artists, these photographers often have a second job to support their work and their lifestyle; it might be in photography or it might involve teaching, working in a museum, or something completely different. These photographers make time for art outside of work.

FREELANCE PHOTOGRAPHY

Freelance photographers run their own businesses. In addition to being great photographers, they need to have business and organizational skills. To get started in business, they need the money to purchase cameras and equipment. To make it run smoothly, they need to understand finances and how to balance the accounts. For the businesses to stay successful, photographers need to build positive relationships with clients.

There are several types of professional photographers. Editorial photographers take pictures for magazines or newspapers. Portrait photographers take pictures of people and at graduations and weddings. Travel photographers venture around the world to capture people and places in images. Other photographers work for advertising agencies or fashion designers, taking photographs to sell products or present styles.

Professional photographers are constantly taking new photographs and experimenting with new technology, skills, perspectives, and other aspects of making images. Photographers are after the best image of a person or a thing in the right moment. It is an ongoing process, whether it is for a client, a customer, or an exhibition.

Like other artists who work in illustration, design, or some form of commercial arts, photographers can also work commercially. Some photographers work as art directors on commercials or film or television sets, deciding how and where to place items so the set looks just right. Other photographers work with video as well as still photography, taking videos of events or making how-to videos.

WHAT IS A PROFESSIONAL PHOTOGRAPHER'S WORK ENVIRONMENT?

Photographers usually work in a combination of settings that includes a studio, sets or locations, a photo lab, and an office or meeting space. Photographers who work for newspapers or magazines spend some of their time in the office, attending meetings and discussing assignments with editors and colleagues. They take photos of events in progress or set up photo shoots in a studio. They also spend time looking at their images and selecting the best one for each job.

Other photographers travel far and wide. In addition to taking photographs, they might be preparing for a journey, researching new equipment, or trekking through a faraway city or remote desert, camera in hand. These photographers

Professional photographers need a certain level of technical knowledge so they know what photographic devices to use and when to use them.

spend some of each year traveling and another part at home, working on books or exhibitions of their work.

HOW IS THE JOB MARKET FOR PROFESSIONAL PHOTOGRAPHERS?

Photography is a popular field with intense competition for jobs. Earnings for professional photographers, as with all jobs in the arts, vary widely. For salaried photographers, those who are employed by a company such as a newspaper or a magazine and receive an annual salary, the Bureau of

Labor reported that the median pay in 2008 was $29,440. Freelance photographers, those who are self-employed and work for a variety of clients, make up more than half of the professional photographers in the United States. They tend to earn slightly less than salaried photographers.[1]

There is no predicted increase in jobs for photographers; digital media has decreased the available work for freelance photographers. Still, available jobs are not expected to decrease either in the coming years.

STOCK PHOTOGRAPHY

You have probably seen stock photographs hundreds of times and may not have known it. Stock photographs are used regularly in books and magazines and on Web sites. For a photograph to sell well in a stock agency, it has to be technically and aesthetically strong. Also, it communicates a message—whether a story, an emotion, or a lifestyle. Look around you—can you pick out what images might be stock photographs? What messages do they convey?

PROFILE OF A PROFESSIONAL PHOTOGRAPHER

Ever since she was a little girl growing up in Louisville, Kentucky, Heather Cantrell knew she wanted to be an artist. She attended an arts magnet high school, and after graduating, attended the Maryland Institute College of Art and declared a major in painting. While in school, she studied in New York, where she started working with mixed media, which eventually led her to photography.

After graduation, Cantrell continued to explore photography. Eventually, she was accepted to graduate school in photography at the University of California Los Angeles (UCLA). At UCLA, she learned to print her own mural-sized images and taught herself how to use a large-format camera.

While supporting herself, Cantrell began working as an assistant to other photographers, learning about the field and making helpful connections. She assisted one photographer who documented artwork and another who took pictures for music magazines. Before long, Cantrell was getting assignments herself, photographing musicians and bands for magazines. Her work appeared in *Spin* and *Index* magazines.

Cantrell liked the intuitive process of taking pictures and enjoyed interacting with the people she photographed. "I've always been very social and have this ability to get people to be comfortable around me and in front of the camera," she said.[2]

While she enjoyed the opportunity to make money by taking pictures, assignments were sporadic. After graduation, Cantrell soon began working in commercials and television. She now works as an art director for reality television shows

"I'm always looking at the monitor and building the set through the lens. I'm not actually taking the picture, but I'm constructing the scene so I'm using the same skill set. I understand lighting—it's built into my vocabulary—and I can work closely with the DP [Director of Photography] because I'm a photographer."[3]

—*Heather Cantrell, photographer, on her work as an art director on* The Bachelor including *The Bachelor* and *The Bachelorette*, which she has worked on since 2007. In this role, Cantrell designs the look of the set and sets up the shots for the camera.

Cantrell has continued to develop her work as an artist. Her most recent group of photographs includes portraits of artists, writers, curators, and others in the art world. This series has been exhibited in Los Angeles, New York, and London.

Cantrell advised young photographers: "Keep an open mind. You never know if you're going to like something until you try it."[4] On a career in photography, Heather stated, "It's always going to change and you have to be open to that, too."[5]

"When I was about twelve, my two most important interests were art and cheese. Since a decadent life in cheese was hard to imagine, I had to convince my middle-class family to support my less exotic choice of art."[6]

—Max Kozloff, photographer, art historian, and critic

A DAY IN THE LIFE OF A PROFESSIONAL PHOTOGRAPHER

Typically, a professional photographer's day-to-day life varies. The photographer's primary tasks include photo shoots, looking carefully at images from a photo shoot and editing them down to the best ones, and developing or producing photographs. In and around these jobs, there is much preparation and communication that must occur for the photographs to be successful. For professional photographers

Some professional photographers travel around the world to take photographs of landscapes, different cultures, and other unique settings.

who are self-employed, they also spend time advertising, networking, and meeting with potential clients.

Once a photographer has a job, preparation includes securing the right equipment, such as specialized lights or lenses, and renting a studio if need be. The photographer also needs to communicate with the client to gain a clear understanding of the photograph's purpose and what it should convey. A photographer's day might include meeting with a client in the morning, attending a photo shoot in the afternoon, and compiling images to send to another client in the evening.

TOP FIVE QUESTIONS ABOUT BECOMING A PROFESSIONAL PHOTOGRAPHER

1. *How do I get started in photography?*

   The best way to get started in photography is by taking pictures. As you take photographs, notice what you see through the lens. How does the light hit the subject? What is and is not included in the frame? Then look carefully at the images after you take them. Pay attention to what worked and what did not work, what you like and what you think could be improved upon.

2. *Where would I work?*

   Photographers work all over the world. They might travel to take photographs of wildlife or islands, or they might travel to local spots to take pictures of weddings or rock bands. But even photographers who have a studio tend to take some photographs on location, such as a garden or a city street.

3. *How would I find work when I'm just starting out?*

   Taking classes or workshops, attending photography exhibitions and lectures, and joining a group or a professional association are ways to meet people in the field and learn about job opportunities. Searching print or electronic ads for jobs is another way to find work, but be aware that newspaper and magazine companies typically require a college or a graduate degree for photography positions.

4. *How would I make a living?*

Many photographers work on a freelance basis, which means they are hired to do various jobs by different clients. Essentially, freelance photographers work for themselves. They must understand how to run a business, which includes finding clients, charging for their work, and developing professional relationships. Another possibility is to become a staff photographer for a magazine or a newspaper. This means that you work full time for one publication, shooting the various images needed for its pages.

5. *Is it difficult to find a job as a photographer?*

Because photography is such a popular field, it is very competitive. The advent of digital photography and the rising availability of cameras likely have made it more competitive. But at the same time, there are more opportunities for images on the Internet. Many photographers rent their best pictures to stock photography houses. These are businesses that rent images for a fee; photographers are paid a percentage when their image is used. Some photographers work as assistants to get to know the business. Others just start taking great pictures and get work by word of mouth.

A photography class can help you build a strong foundation of skills.

WOULD YOU MAKE A GOOD PROFESSIONAL PHOTOGRAPHER?

There are all kinds of professional photographers, but it's safe to say that the majority of them share an enjoyment in the process of taking pictures and a curiosity about the world and how to capture its many facets in an image. Take a look at some of the other key skills and traits professional photographers have to see if you may someday be a great photographer.

TECHNICAL KNOWLEDGE

Professional photographers have a high level of technical knowledge about the field and the ability to work with computers and digital imagery. Many photographers benefit from a background or training in art. This can develop an important awareness of composition, the use of light, the importance of angles, and the ideas behind images.

FLEXIBILITY

Because photography is a challenging career that does not follow a singular route to success, it's helpful to be an adventurous self-starter. If you prefer routine and stability, this might not be the best career choice for you. Even in a staff photography job, every day brings

ONE ROUTE TO PHOTOGRAPHY

In the 1920s and 1930s, the artist Man Ray revolutionized photography by inventing a new process for making images that did not require a camera. He called his pictures rayographs. These were made by exposing images and objects on photographic paper directly to a single light source for a short time. Man Ray was an important surrealist artist and a founder of the Dada movement, which included artists who challenged the status quo of both art and society. Ray started out as a painter, but he essentially gave it up for photography, though at that time, very few artists worked in photography.

something new. Photographers have to be able to handle—even enjoy—change, adventure, and variety.

CALM UNDER PRESSURE

Most professional photographers need to work well under pressure. Photographers on staff at newspapers or magazines are under deadline pressures constantly and cover local assignments, such as a parade or an awards ceremony. At the national level, photographers sometimes cover dangerous, pivotal, or once-in-a-lifetime events. Brave and street-smart photographers that are able to keep their wits about them and perform well under a variety of circumstances would do well in this field. Freelance photographers face the same kind of deadline pressure during projects, but they may have more time and ability to create the perfect lighting and environment for each shot.

"All photographs are accurate; none of them is the truth."[1]

—Richard Avedon (1923–2004), prominent portrait and fashion photographer

BUSINESS AND PEOPLE SKILLS

Since the majority of professional photographers are freelance and operate their own businesses, a certain amount of business and marketing skills are useful for a successful photography career. If you know how to stick to a budget, track finances, and gather resources, freelance photography could be a good fit for you.

Being able to take great photographs is only one part of being a successful professional photographer. You will also need good people skills and determination.

Photographers need to be able to work well with people, especially their clients. The ability to make people feel comfortable during a photo shoot is a necessary trait. People skills also help build and keep a clientele.

CHECKLIST

Maybe you are sure you are interested in photography, but you're still not sure if it's the right career path. The following questions will help you reflect on your unique talents and interests as you begin to consider whether photography is the right career for you.

- *Do you love taking and looking at photographs?*

- *Have you ever noticed the way light hits objects and affects setting and mood?*

- *Are you energetic, adventurous, and a self-starter?*

- *Do you like day-to-day life to hold variety?*

- *Do you often take photographs at family functions?*

If you answered yes to most of these questions, photography may be a career path for you. Even if you answered no to some of the questions, photography may still be a possible career path for you. Take some time to explore why you might want to be a professional photographer and what skills you would need to develop. Hard work and perseverance can go a long way in finding and following a career path.

HOW TO GET THERE

EDUCATION

If photography classes are offered at your school, take those. This will provide you with a good foundation of basic photography skills upon which you can build throughout your career. While photography courses are crucial, other classes can aid a budding photographer. These include film and video, new media, art history, painting and drawing, the history of photography, world cultures, and basic math or economics. Depending on what type of photography you want to pursue, classes in politics, geography, environmental studies, music, literature, and journalism could be beneficial. Take classes that interest you because you never know if a subject you're passionate about could be a potential photography path.

> ## PHOTOGRAPHY AND WRITING
>
> One way to break into photography is to hone your writing skills along with your photographic vision. Small magazines and local papers are often happy to get the photos and text for stories from one source. It can save them money and get you published. A savvy photographer who can also write is usually a win-win situation for a publisher.

Today, most photographers go from high school into college and sometimes even to graduate school. Some study in specialized schools for photography, art, journalism, or new media. Others attend public universities or community colleges. While all jobs in photography do not always require a college degree, having one will make you far more competitive and expand your options in the field. You may also consider taking a class or a workshop on business management for artists. Several arts-related organizations offer these.

UNDERSTANDING TECHNOLOGY

There is much more to photography than simply taking pictures. Professional photographers need to stay informed about the ever-advancing technology in their field and have a strong understanding of photographic equipment, computers, and imaging software. Perhaps you already have a computer. You can start exploring an image software program and experiment with the different ways it alters images. Think about how each change impacts the meaning and sensibility of the photograph.

STUDY ON YOUR OWN

You can be on your way to becoming a professional photographer by observing what is

EXPLORE YOUR CURRENT SURROUNDINGS

Look around! You might find exactly the subject you are looking to photograph. Some of the most well-known photographers have developed their vision and body of work right in the area where they live. Photographers including American Diane Arbus and Frenchman Henri Cartier Bresson each found the inspiration and subjects for their uniquely captivating subjects in the people and places around them.

Practice your photography skills by taking lots of photographs. Afterward, analyze your pictures to see the things you did well and the areas you can improve upon.

around you. Observe the way light hits everyday objects. Notice the way light affects mood and changes throughout the day. You can also hold up your hands and frame potential photos to practice the process of constructing an image. What's included in each picture is as important as what's excluded.

Take time to look carefully at photographs, too. Look at images you like and those you do not like. Look at images that interest you, that you find dull, and everything in between. Try to determine where the light is coming from in each picture and what type of light source illuminates the frame. Consider why some photographs are successful and others are not. Explain them to someone or write them down. Being able to take the ideas in your head and turn them into words allows you to converse intelligently with others about photography.

It's also important to spend time considering the purpose of the images you see. What was the photographer's intent? Do you think it was for a job or a work of art? Does the photograph tell a story, sell a product, or convince you of an idea? As you understand more about photography, you will begin to have a better sense of the photographs you want to take and how they can contribute to the web of images all around you. Beginning to see and think like a professional photographer will put you closer to your goal.

Professional photographers must be patient and accurate in order to capture an image of a scene that passes quickly.

Curators in large museums may have specific types of art they are in charge of overseeing.

WHAT IS A CURATOR?

A curator is someone who works in a museum or works independently to organize and oversee art exhibitions. Curators who work in museums are called museum curators or institutional curators. They have full-time, salaried positions. Institutional curators normally specialize in one area, for example, in African art, contemporary art, or photography. They present exhibitions and oversee the collection of their area of expertise.

Institutional curators organize shows and also oversee a museum's collection—the body of art that the museum owns. The curator makes suggestions as to how to care for, exhibit, and expand the collection. A curator does extensive research to support each recommendation with a written and verbal presentation to the museum board. In addition to researching and planning exhibitions, curators often oversee fund-raising for the institution, apply for grants, and meet with artists and collectors. They may travel to other cities' museums to view their exhibitions, write catalog essays, and devise programs and literature to reach out to the public and make the museum accessible to more people.

Independent curators do not plan and organize exhibitions for one institution; rather,

TRAVELING THE WORLD

Curating can take you around the world. Hou Hanru, a successful curator from China, currently lives and works in the United States. Hanru has lived in France and curated exhibitions in cities all over the world, including Istanbul, Amsterdam, Paris, and Venice.

they propose exhibitions to museums and galleries and present exhibitions in various venues. Independent curators, like artists, work on a freelance basis. They often also have other jobs, including writing for art magazines and journals, working as artists themselves, or sometimes advising collectors on what art to purchase. While independent curators may not receive a steady paycheck, they may prefer the flexibility and variety of independent work.

Artists, writers, and historians can all hold curatorial jobs. Traditionally, museum curator positions have required a doctoral degree in art history, but increasingly, a master's degree in fine art, art history, or a related field is acceptable for these positions.

WHAT IS A CURATOR'S WORK ENVIRONMENT?

Curators work in museums or in other institutions, such as prominent art collections or libraries that hold important, archival materials. Some curators work independently or in collaboration with art galleries, museums, or nonprofit exhibition spaces.

Curators working in museums are responsible for organizing exhibitions and maintaining the museums' collections. At the museums, curators research; write proposals, essays, and other materials for exhibitions; and work with their colleagues. But some of the curators' work is done outside the museums to meet with artists, collectors, and donors. They may also attend exhibitions at other museums and galleries. Curators' colleagues in museums include archivists, conservators, preparators, and museum educators.

In smaller museums, there is sometimes only one curator who organizes all of the exhibitions. These curators are usually called museum directors because they oversee all of the major functions of the museum. These curators have more administrative duties than curators of specialized areas in larger museums. Directors oversee staff, interns, and volunteers as well as administering the museums' day-to-day functioning.

DEFENDING ART CHOICES

In July 2010, after a nearly three-year trial, Russian curators Yury Samodurov and Andrei Yerofeyev were fined for mounting an exhibition that was perceived as offensive to religion. The show in question, "Forbidden Art," included works that had been banned from museum exhibitions and was intended to challenge censorship of art. One work featured an image of Jesus Christ as Mickey Mouse. Yerofeyev explained that it was intended to show how a child might perceive these two figures, overlapping their importance, but others saw it as offensive.

HOW IS THE JOB MARKET FOR CURATORS?

Jobs are competitive in all areas of the arts, and curatorial positions are no different. A curator is one of the rare salaried positions in the art world. (Other salaried positions include teaching or arts administration.) Before obtaining a full-time position, curators often spend years working at part-time, volunteer, or intern positions for additional training and experience. Although it's a competitive area, jobs for curators are expected to grow between now and 2018, due in part to increased museum attendance.

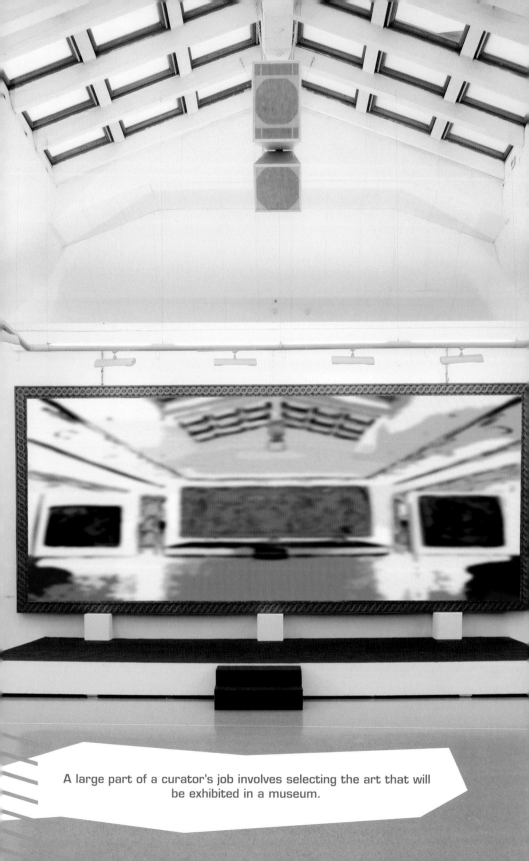

A large part of a curator's job involves selecting the art that will be exhibited in a museum.

The Bureau of Labor Statistics reported the median wage for museum curators to be $47,220. On the lower end of the pay scale, some curators made between $27,000 and $35,300. On the upper end, some curators made more than $80,000.[1]

The demand for independent curators has been on the rise in recent years, and the prospects are good for continued growth. Independent curators are paid through grants, museums, or institutions. Some work for no fee to gain experience. The rates vary but tend to be lower, relative to the amount of time spent on the job, than salaried curators.

A PROFILE OF A CURATOR

Julie Joyce has always been interested in art and academics. As a child, she excelled in art classes but changed course in high school after receiving a lesser grade in art. "I couldn't risk my GPA declining by continuing to take art and receiving bad grades," Joyce explained.[2] So she left art behind for a time.

In college, Joyce took art classes again, including art history for the first time. On a class visit to the Museum of Contemporary Art in Los Angeles, an exhibition of paintings by Mark Rothko took Joyce's breath away. She remembered,

> I didn't understand them and couldn't think of the precise reason they affected me so deeply. But I realized I wanted to know more. The next day I changed my major to Art History, not knowing exactly where this would lead, but with the resolve that I wanted to work with art in some way and therefore needed to know more about it.[3]

During college, Joyce volunteered at a museum and learned about the job of a curator. She volunteered in the Registrar's Department and worked directly with objects in the museum, such as ancient costumes and nineteenth-century prints. Entranced by the museum, she spent her breaks wandering through exhibitions, wondering about the intentions and lives of the artists behind the work on the walls.

After college, she searched persistently for a job in a gallery and landed a position as a registrar and administrative assistant in a reputable gallery. Of this experience, she said,

"Curating is a great challenge and I often think of it as solving a puzzle. I put together various pieces in just the right way to tell a story or to express a point of view, whether it's my perspective or the artist's. I'm able to share these stories by writing essays regarding artists and exhibition ideas and lecturing to students and museum visitors."[5]

—Julie Joyce, curator of contemporary art,
Santa Barbara Museum of Art

In the six and a half years I was there, I learned more about the contemporary art world than I ever thought was possible, mostly by working directly with art and meeting many of the people involved in driving the contemporary art world: artists, collectors, art dealers, museum staff, writers, and more.[4]

Joyce decided to return to school to become a curator. After receiving her master's degree, she worked her way up from part-time jobs in smaller museums to full-time

WHAT IS A CURATOR?

curatorial work, and eventually to her current position, the curator of contemporary art at Santa Barbara Museum of Art, where she is in charge of the collection and exhibitions of contemporary art.

One of her favorite things about being a curator is "the opportunity to meet and interact with artists," Joyce said.[6] She also enjoys the variety:

> Each day can be very different, which is what helps make my job exciting. On some days, I will go into the office and meet with my colleagues regarding upcoming programs, perhaps have lunch with a potential donor or visiting colleague, and, in the afternoon, maybe lecture to a museum group either in our lecture halls or in front of the work in the galleries.[7]

On the days that she is not in the gallery, Joyce visits artists' studios, collectors' homes, or other museum exhibitions. Often, she travels to other cities, particularly in Europe, to see what is happening in the art world there.

"I am passionate about what I do for a living—working

"Being a curator is using pattern repetition. You see one thing happening here and another thing happening there and you start to sense a new swelling wave of something going on. You build an exhibition around it to take a pulse of the current moment. . . . It's like throwing down the gauntlet and saying, 'This is important and we should pay attention to it—we should champion or recognize these artists.'"[8]

—Michael Darling, *curator, Seattle Art Museum*

with art and working in a museum," Joyce stated. "It's a unique environment where I am surrounded by things I truly appreciate and people who I enjoy learning from."[9]

A DAY IN THE LIFE OF A CURATOR

Many curators, like Joyce, work in museums. A typical day includes being in the museum, preparing exhibitions, meeting with colleagues, writing related exhibition materials, giving lectures or talks, and communicating with artists or other institutions, both for research and in the development of exhibitions.

But curators do not spend all their time at the museums. A typical day could also include traveling to meet with artists in their studios, to look at art exhibitions in other museums and galleries, or to meet with donors and collectors.

Curators meet with artists, donors, and other museum
employees to set up exhibitions.

TOP FIVE QUESTIONS ABOUT BECOMING A CURATOR

1. *How do I find a job as a curator?*

    These competitive jobs almost always require a graduate degree, most often a doctorate, such as a PhD in art history. More recently, curators who have a master's degree and experience in a museum are also being hired as curators. Plan on doing volunteer work, job shadowing, and working your way up to a curator position.

2. *What is the difference between a museum curator and an independent curator?*

    Museum curators work for one institution; they receive a salary and are committed to representing the interests of the museum where they work. Independent curators work on a freelance basis. They organize exhibitions according to their personal interests and present these ideas to various institutions. Sometimes independent curators, also called guest curators, are well-known artists, writers, or celebrities who bring attention to an institution or an exhibition.

3. *Who curates the shows in art galleries?*

    A gallery director, also referred to as an art dealer or a dealer due to their role as a salesperson of art, is an individual who owns a gallery that exhibits and sells art. Gallery directors usually decide what to show in their spaces. Sometimes, they work with independent or guest curators. Gallery directors represent a roster of artists and include their work in exhibitions and promote their work to collectors and curators.

4. *Could I work outside an art museum?*

Curators can work in history museums, museums for science and industry, and environmental and nature centers. Independent curators work with galleries, nonprofit organizations, college and university art galleries, and sometimes with venues that are not related to art, such as hospitals or corporations, to display art.

5. *As a curator, how would I select the art to exhibit?*

A curator's interests, research, experience, and the topic or location of the exhibition can play a role in what is included. For example, if an exhibition is on ancient Indian art, the curator would do research and likely travel to India to meet with scholars, museum curators, and researchers in the area to determine what is available for loan and what would be important and interesting to include. For a more contemporary exhibition, the curator might determine what the current trends or sensibilities are and arrange an exhibition around these ideas or highlight who he or she views as an underrepresented artist.

Students who excel in academics and enjoy thinking about art may fit well in a curator's position.

WOULD YOU MAKE A GOOD CURATOR?

Good curators are skilled at research, writing, looking, listening, and reflecting. Effective curators consider the motivations, practices, and expressions of artists, living and dead, and need to be able to understand what an artist was trying to achieve. Take a look at some of the other key skills and traits curators share to see if being a curator would fit well with who you are.

EXCEL IN ACADEMICS

Curatorial positions require higher education, and a person with a degree in the liberal arts and humanities would be an asset to this job. Curators attend school for many years and then spend time researching and writing on the job. Curators also need to be creative and articulate. They must imagine what they want to present and articulate these ideas clearly, in discussion and in writing.

> "It's so much easier to write with intelligence, I think, about what you're viewing if you know the *history* of what you're viewing and how it was arrived at. The progression of moves the artists have personally made to get from where they were to where they are."[2]
>
> —*John Coplans (1920–2003), artist, critic, and a founder of* Artforum

OBSERVANT AND THOUGHTFUL

Curators are curious in general and particularly curious about art and its impact on society and culture. Curator Julie Joyce stated,

> A good curator is also a keen observer. The best curators that I know are open-minded and take time to really look at art—not just seeing, but also taking the time to study it, to ponder it.[1]

87

This level of looking and thinking about art is important. Curators do not simply exhibit the work they like; they also exhibit the work they believe is important, culturally and historically. Curators aim to add something new to the dialogue of art.

COMMUNICATING AND WORKING WITH OTHERS

Even though curators are responsible for exhibitions, they spend a lot of time communicating with others, including artists, donors, museum staff and patrons, and students of the arts. The ability to communicate and work effectively with others is beneficial for curators. If you enjoy working with others on projects and are energized by the conversations and ideas inspired by different points of view, then you will probably work well in a museum environment.

"Well, the only thing, no matter if [viewers] think it is good or bad, is that they go out with an extra tool to think about their own stories or their own lives. I think that's the purpose of museums or shows—people go in, and they come out with something more, with an extra element in their mind or in their spirit to look at their reality from a different point of view."[3]

—Francesco Bonami, curator, critic, and writer

CHECKLIST

The following questions will help you determine if being a curator is the job for you. Included in these questions are prompts that will help you understand your skills and strengths. Be honest in your responses; reflecting on them can help you decide if you want to be a curator.

- Do you like school and normally get good grades?

- Are you a strong writer, and do you enjoy writing?

- Do you enjoy researching topics for papers?

- Do you like looking at and discussing art?

- Are you interested in communicating your ideas about art and culture?

- Do you prefer to look at art, as opposed to making it?

- Do you enjoy working with others on group projects?

If you answered yes to most of these questions, curating may be a career path for you. If you answered no to some of the questions, a curator still may be a position for you. Take some time to discover your deeper interests and skills you could learn. Do these coincide with those of a curator?

Curators think about artists' motivations for their work.

HOW TO GET THERE

EDUCATION AND EXPERIENCE

Becoming a curator takes time and education. Classes that relate to becoming a curator include art, art history, film, philosophy, history, visual studies, literature, writing, and political science. Because the majority of museum curators have PhDs in art history or a related field, it is important to get good grades and plan on going to college and graduate school. A PhD is the highest educational degree possible and

> "My job is to keep people focused on the hundred and one artists that are in my show."[4]
>
> —*Robert Storr, curator, critic, and dean of Yale School of Art*

takes time to achieve, but some curators work with master's degrees and even, at times, bachelor's degrees.

VOLUNTEER AND INTERN

Many curators have put in a lot of time as volunteers in museums. Contact your local museum or art center and ask if there are any volunteer positions or internships that you can apply for, if not now then as you get older. Internships and volunteer positions are a great way to learn about art and museums and to meet people in the field. In *Careers in Art*, author Blythe Camenson pointed out,

> Whatever your course of study, most museums require an upper-level degree, either in an academic discipline or

If you want to be a curator, become involved in the art world by exploring and volunteering at museums.

in *museum studies, museum science, or museology. An intensive internship or record of long-term volunteer work is also required.*[5]

EXPLORE THE ART WORLD

Curators spend a good deal of time on research, which includes visiting different museums and exploring the current art scene. One of the best ways to start down the path to become a curator is to learn as much as you can about art and art history. Attending museum and gallery exhibitions is a great way to learn more about art. Ask your parents or teachers to arrange a trip to a museum or gallery in your community. Pay attention to the different kinds of shows featured at different museums and galleries. Take time to read related publications and texts. Try to understand how the curator made choices about what to include and what the exhibition is meant to say or to show you.

Another route for exploration is an informational interview with a curator. This can even be done by e-mail if

"I would encourage young people to expose themselves to art—ask their parents to take them to museums or to art galleries, not just in your home-town but also when you travel to other cities. Art refers not just to art from the past, but also to all kinds of subjects, like history, literature, and all kinds of cultural phenomenon. It can be fun trying to figure out what a work of art means together or even on your own."[6]

—*Julie Joyce, curator of contemporary art, Santa Barbara Museum of Art* the curator does not have time to meet in person. Ask about the curator's education and experience. You might also ask for any advice for someone just starting along his or her career path.

ORGANIZE ART SHOWS

Try organizing your own art show by putting together a show of artwork from your school or community. It may not be easy to find a space to show art, but be creative. Talk to your teachers about setting up an exhibition at the school. Consider the possibility of organizing a show in a local café or at a community center or a youth group meeting hall.

When you decide what to exhibit, begin by looking at what your friends and classmates are making, but look beyond that, too. See what students in other classes are working on and what kind of art is being made in your community. Perhaps you will organize an exhibition of an artist from a local senior citizen's home or by a student in your school who is a great painter. Sometimes the best ideas for exhibitions come as a surprise; art involves a sense of discovery.

Curators must be able to communicate and work well with others, including preparators, to keep museums running smoothly.

GET YOUR FOOT IN THE DOOR

The main way to get your foot in the door in the arts is to participate. This includes making, performing, or studying the arts as well as attending performances and exhibitions. Learn as much as you can as both an artist and an audience member. Also, join the art club at your school, and if there isn't one, start one. Discussing and creating art with a group of your peers will be a good learning experience—not to mention fun!

Job shadowing an artist or someone who is in the arts is a great way to see the day-to-day activities of a job you're interested in. You'll be able to ask questions and glean some advice on how that person was able to reach his or her position. If you have a friend, a relative, or a teacher involved in the art form that interests you, ask this person to recommend friends or colleagues who might allow you to shadow them for an afternoon to learn about the job.

If you do get the opportunity to shadow someone in the arts, be respectful of the fact that the person has let you into his or her life, work, and art for a time. Listen to what he or she has to say, observe what he or she does, and always be courteous. Remember to thank the person, both verbally and with a handwritten thank-you note. If professional associations have meetings in your area, you could volunteer to do registration or other administrative tasks for the meeting and possibly be able to listen to, and even talk to, the speakers.

Another way to get your foot in the door is to seek out a mentor, an invaluable resource to have as you travel along your career path. This person can provide you with feedback on your art, answer questions you have, and help you prepare your portfolio. He or she will probably have a lot to teach you about the art world, too. Learning from a mentor will help you become a better artist, and your mentor may also help you network with other professionals.

Museums, galleries, and other arts organizations often have intern or volunteer opportunities. Check with your local cultural institutions to find out what opportunities are available and what qualifications are needed to apply to intern or volunteer. Because of the competitive nature of the arts, it is challenging to land internships, particularly at high-profile art galleries and museums. Employers will expect a professional résumé and well-written cover letter when you apply for an internship. Your qualifications, research, and polite persistence are the keys to landing internships. Internship and volunteer experiences are key ways to meet people and network within the arts industry.

PROFESSIONAL ORGANIZATIONS

You might want to contact some of the following professional organizations for more information on the jobs in this book.

ARTIST

Alliance of Professional Artists
www.allproartists.org/home.asp

American Art Therapy Association
www.arttherapy.org

National Art Education Association
www.naea-reston.org

PROFESSIONAL DANCER

American Dance Therapy Association
www.adta.org

National Dance Teachers Association of America
www.nationaldanceteachers.org

Performing Arts Alliance
http://theperformingartsalliance.org/site/
PageServer?pagename=paa_home_page

Stage Directors and Choreographers Society
http://sdcweb.org

PROFESSIONAL PHOTOGRAPHER

American Society of Media Photographers
http://asmp.org

Art Director's Club
www.adcglobal.org

National Press Photographer's Association
www.nppa.org

Professional Photographers of America
www.ppa.com

CURATOR

Art Dealers Association of America
www.artdealers.org

Association of Art Museum Curators
www.artcurators.org

Independent Curators International
www.ici-exhibitions.org

MARKET FACTS

JOB	NUMBER OF JOBS	GROWTH RATE	
Artist	221,900	*average*	
Professional Dancer	29,200 (includes choreographers)	*more slowly than average*	
Professional Photographer	152,000	*average*	
Curator	11,700	*much faster than average*	

MEDIAN WAGE	RELATED JOBS	SKILLS
$42,650 per year	art teacher, commercial artist, preparator	creative, passionate, resilient, self-motivated
$12.22 per hour for dancers; $38,520 per year for choreographers	dance teacher, choreographer, yoga and Pilates instructor	disciplined, energetic, fit, perseverant
$29,440 per year	art director	business skills, calm under pressure, people skills, technical knowledge
$47,220 per year	archivist, conservator, museum educator	excel in academics, passionate about art, people skills, thoughtful

All statistics from the *Bureau of Labor Statistics Occupational Outlook Handbook, 2010–2011 Edition*

GLOSSARY

art
Work made by an artist that is intended to be seen, considered, and reflected upon.

art director
A commercial art job in advertising, graphic design, or film and television that involves supervising or directing other creative professionals and overseeing the look of a product, set, image, or other product being made.

choreographer
An individual who arranges, composes, and directs a dance.

collector
A person who purchases art and maintains an art collection; usually an individual who has a passion for art and wants to support the arts and artists.

company
A group, association, or troupe of dancers who perform and collaborate on dances, usually under the direction of a choreographer or an artistic director.

donor

A person who donates money or other resources to a museum or an institution.

grants

Private or governmental monies given to artists to develop their work.

networking

Connecting with people and developing relationships that will impact business.

portfolio

A selection of images representing an artist's body of work.

residencies

Places where artists can live and work on their art for a period of time.

ADDITIONAL RESOURCES

FURTHER READINGS

Bell-Rehwoldt, Sheri. *Careers for the Twenty-First Century: Art.* Detroit, MI: Lucent, 2005. Print.

Bhandari, Darcy Heather, and Jonathan Melber. *Art/Work: Everything You Need to Know (and Do) As You Pursue Your Art Career.* New York: Free Press, 2009. Print.

Burdick, Jan E. *Creative Careers in Museums.* New York: Allworth, 2008. Print.

Ferguson, ed. *Careers in Focus: Art.* New York: Ferguson, 2008. Print.

Gilbert, George, and Pamela Fehl. *Career Opportunities in Photography.* New York: Ferguson, 2006. Print.

Nathan, Amy. *Meet the Dancers: From Ballet, Broadway, and Beyond.* New York: Henry Holt, 2008. Print.

Orenstein, Vik. *The Photographer's Market Guide to Building Your Photography Business.* Cincinnati, OH: Writer's Digest, 2009. Print.

Paul, Tina. *So You Want to Dance on Broadway?: Insight and Advice from the Pros Who Know.* Portsmouth, NH: Heinemann, 2003. Print.

Reeves, Diane Lindsey. *Career Ideas for Teens in the Arts and Communications*. New York: Ferguson, 2005. Print.

Schlatter, N. Elizabeth. *Museum Careers: A Practical Guide for Novices and Students*. Walnut Creek, CA: Left Coast, 2008. Print.

WEB LINKS

To learn more about jobs in the arts, visit ABDO Publishing Company online at **www.abdopublishing.com**. Web sites about jobs in the arts are featured on our Book Links page. These links are routinely monitored and updated to provide the most current information available.

SOURCE NOTES

CHAPTER 1. IS AN ARTS JOB FOR YOU?

1. Keith Haring. *Keith Haring Journals*. New York: Penguin, 1997. Print. 12.

2. Office of Research & Analysis. "Artists in the Workforce: 1990–2005." *NEA.gov*. National Endowment for the Arts, May 2008. Web. 21 Sept. 2010.

3. Frances Morris, ed. *Louise Bourgeois*. Los Angeles: Museum of Contemporary Art, 2007. Print. 111.

4. U.S. Bureau of Labor Statistics. "Artists and Related Workers." *Occupational Outlook Handbook, 2010–11 Edition*. U.S. Bureau of Labor Statistics, 17 Dec. 2009. Web. 21 Sept. 2010.

5. Ibid.

6. Blythe Camenson. *Careers in Art*. New York: McGraw Hill, 2007. Print. 1.

7. "Arts Education Facts." *The Arts: Ask for More*. Americans for the Arts, 24 Feb. 2009. Web. 21 Sept. 2010.

CHAPTER 2. WHAT IS AN ARTIST?

1. David Humphrey. *Blind Handshake*. New York: Periscope, 2009. Print. 25.

2. Sarah Thornton. *Seven Days in the Art World*. New York: Norton, 2008. Print. 199.

3. Heather Darcy Bhandari and Jonathan Melber. *Art/Work*. New York: Free Press, 2009. Print. 18.

4. U.S. Bureau of Labor Statistics. "Artists and Related Workers." *Occupational Outlook Handbook, 2010–11 Edition*. U.S. Bureau of Labor Statistics, 17 Dec. 2009. Web. 21 Sept. 2010.

5. Heather Darcy Bhandari and Jonathan Melber. *Art/Work*. New York: Free Press, 2009. Print. 18.

6. U.S. Bureau of Labor Statistics. "Artists and Related Workers." *Occupational Outlook Handbook, 2010–11 Edition*. U.S. Bureau of Labor Statistics, 17 Dec. 2009. Web. 21 Sept. 2010.

7. Dane Picard. Interview by A. M. Buckley. July 2010.

8. Ibid.

9. Ibid.

CHAPTER 3. WOULD YOU MAKE A GOOD ARTIST?

1. Dane Picard. Interview by A. M. Buckley. July 2010.

2. Heather Darcy Bhandari and Jonathan Melber. *Art/Work*. New York: Free Press, 2009. Print. 7.

3. Heather Cantrell. Interview by A. M. Buckley. 6 July 2010.

4. U.S. Bureau of Labor Statistics. "Artists and Related Workers." *Occupational Outlook Handbook, 2010–11 Edition*. U.S. Bureau of Labor Statistics, 17 Dec. 2009. Web. 21 Sept. 2010.

5. Sarah Thornton. *Seven Days in the Art World*. New York: Norton, 2008. Print. 37.

6. Helen Stoilas. "Robert Storr: Most theory has little bearing on art." *The Art Newspaper*. The Art Newspaper, 2010. Web. 16 Oct. 2009.

CHAPTER 4. WHAT IS A PROFESSIONAL DANCER?

1. Elaina Loveland. *Creative Careers*. Los Altos, CA: SuperCollege, 2007. Print. 203.

2. U.S. Bureau of Labor Statistics. "Dancers and Choreographers." *Occupational Outlook Handbook, 2010–11 Edition*. U.S. Bureau of Labor Statistics, 17 Dec. 2009. Web. 21 Sept. 2010.

3. Elaine Wang. Interview by A. M. Buckley. 4 July 2010.

4. U.S. Bureau of Labor Statistics. "Dancers and Choreographers." *Occupational Outlook Handbook, 2010–11 Edition*. U.S. Bureau of Labor Statistics, 17 Dec. 2009. Web. 21 Sept. 2010.

5. Elaine Wang. Interview by A. M. Buckley. 4 July 2010.

6. Ibid.

7. Ibid.

8. Ibid.

9. Ibid.

10. Dean Speer and Francis Timlin. "International Contracting and Releasing: An Interview with Martha Graham Dance Company Soloist Tadej Brdnik." *CriticalDance.com*. CriticalDance.com, n.d. Web. 21 Sept. 2010.

SOURCE NOTES CONTINUED

CHAPTER 5. WOULD YOU MAKE A GOOD PROFESSIONAL DANCER?

1. Elaina Loveland. *Creative Careers*. Los Altos, CA: SuperCollege, 2007. Print. 181.

2. Ibid. 183.

3. Elaine Wang. Interview with A. M. Buckley. 4 July 2010.

CHAPTER 6. WHAT IS A PROFESSIONAL PHOTOGRAPHER?

1. U.S. Bureau of Labor Statistics. "Photographers." *Occupational Outlook Handbook, 2010–11 Edition*. U.S. Bureau of Labor Statistics, 17 Dec. 2009. Web. 21 Sept. 2010.

2. Heather Cantrell. Interview by A. M. Buckley. 6 July 2010.

3. Ibid.

4. Ibid.

5. Ibid.

6. Amy Newman. *Challenging Art: Artforum 1962-1974*. New York: Soho, 2000. Print. 53.

CHAPTER 7. WOULD YOU MAKE A GOOD PROFESSIONAL PHOTOGRAPHER?

1. An Avedon Portrait. PBS Online NewsHour. Interview by Jeffrey Brown. *PBS.org*. PBS, 24 Oct. 2002. Web. 21 Sept. 2010.

CHAPTER 8. WHAT IS A CURATOR?

1. U.S. Bureau of Labor Statistics. "Archivists, Curators, and Museum Technicians." *Occupational Outlook Handbook, 2010–11 Edition*. U.S. Bureau of Labor Statistics, 17 Dec. 2009. Web. 21 Sept. 2010.

2. Julie Joyce. Interview by A. M. Buckley. July 2010.

3. Ibid.

4. Ibid.

5. Ibid.

6. Ibid.

7. Ibid.

8. Heather Darcy Bhandari and Jonathan Melber. *Art/Work*. New York: Free Press, 2009. Print. 6.

9. Julie Joyce. Interview by A. M. Buckley. July 2010.

CHAPTER 9. WOULD YOU MAKE A GOOD CURATOR?

1. Julie Joyce. Interview by A. M. Buckley. July 2010.

2. Amy Newman. *Challenging Art: Artforum 1962–1974*. New York: Soho, 2000. Print. 93.

3. Lisa Phillips. "Whitney Biennial." *InterviewMagazine.com*. Interview Magazine, n.d. Web. 21 Sept. 2010.

4. Sarah Thornton. *Seven Days in the Art World*. New York: Norton, 2008. Print. 229.

5. Blythe Camenson. *Careers in Art*. New York: McGraw Hill, 2007. Print. 79.

6. Julie Joyce. Interview by A. M. Buckley. July 2010.

INDEX

ABOUT THE AUTHOR

A. M. Buckley is an artist, writer, editor, and educator based in Los Angeles. She is the author of several nonfiction books for children. Her writing about contemporary art appears regularly on Artforum.com and in magazines, including *Art in America*, and she is the former editor in chief of *Artweek*. Her art has been included in numerous group and solo exhibitions since 1993 at venues including Carl Berg Gallery and Jancar Gallery in Los Angeles. Buckley is a graduate of University of California, Berkeley and received a Master's in Fine Art from Otis College of Art and Design.

PHOTO CREDITS